Seasons Change, So Do We

Jocelyn Lansangan

BookLeaf
Publishing

Presentation by *BookLeaf Publishing*

Web: www.bookleafpub.com

E-mail: info@bookleafpub.com

ISBN: 9789357442763

First edition 2023

For you

For me

For us all

- jpl

ACKNOWLEDGEMENT

First, I'd like to thank my parents, Ester and Soliven Lansangan Sr. Through all the pain, there was and is also so much love. I'm grateful for the sacrifices you both made to try and make a better life for yourselves and your families.

I love you so much, mom. Thank you for giving me life. For teaching me the importance of kindness, bravery and to have/keep a good heart.

To my Sissy and Brother, I love you guys so much. I honestly don't know where I'd be without you guys. Thank you for always being there. My heart soars that you both found your person who are equally amazing as the both of you. Love all of you!

To my heart, hanai and fam bam ‘ohana, thank you all for giving me a home when I didn't feel safe in mine. You saved me.

To my friends (especially my girls), I love you all more than you’ll ever know and cherish each of our friendships.

Thank you all for the love, laughs, and all the memories that I'll never forget, and cheers to the many more that'll come.

Thank you to Book Leaf Publishing for this amazing opportunity.

Thank you to you, whoever is reading this. I hope my words can help you on your healing journey in this beautiful, chaotic thing we call life. You can do this. Don't give up.

Most of all, thank you to my flower. The light I never knew I needed, but God did, and blessed me with you. You inspire me everyday and I'm so grateful for you. I love you to the moon and back, kid.

PREFACE

To anyone who is in pain,

You're not alone. You will overcome this.
You're not the only one broken. We all are. But, there is a certain beauty in brokenness. Knowing that we can help one another by picking up each others pieces.

We're not meant to do life alone. So, please remember that there is always another way. Don't succumb to the darkness. Reach out for the light.

Remember, seasons change. As do we.

Sincerely,
Jocelyn Paras Lansangan
(A Kindred Spirit)

Asylum

They say the definition of insanity is to do the same thing over and over again, expecting to yield different results.

By this definition, I would say 90% of the population is crazy.

And yet, it is the 10%
Those who are willing to take risks
Those who are willing to be different
Those who believe they can turn the impossible into possible
Those who create change
That are deemed insane.

They are ostracized
Criticized
Sometimes even
Lobotomized

To the asylum they are sent
With all the other dreamers
I'm sorry, I mean
Crazies.

-jpl

Forgotten

She made sure to leave traces of herself
everywhere
Rubber bands and bobby pins throughout the
house
Books shoved in dressers and cabinet drawers
Little notes she wrote her random thoughts on
And grocery lists scattered everywhere
Most people would think that she was just a
messy, careless, forgetful person
But little do they know she did this on purpose
Placing things where they should not be
Not because she was forgetful
But because she didn't want to be
forgotten

-jpl

Chinatown

There are the drunks again
who would holler from inside and outside the bars
at 11 in the morning to an 11-year-old girl
Trying to touch her so often that she learned to walk on the other side of the street
The side with less bars and less drunks

6 years later, her bus passes her mom's store just as it always does each morning
She looks out the window to catch sight of her
just as she always does each morning
Yes, there she is
She looks okay
The girl puts her head down and continues to do her homework
Until she gets off three stops later to get to class

3 years later she walks comfortably to her mother's store
to surprise her with the flowers she's just picked up for her from the corner store
A homeless man tells her to zip her purse up
because someone might steal her belongings
She zips up her purse and thanks him

She then makes her way to the opposite side of
the street
The one with less bars and less drunks
To have lunch with her best friends at the new
restaurant that has just opened up

Then she crosses the street again
The one where drunken hands had once tried to
pull on her pigtails
But this time instead goes into her favorite
coffee shop to order her usual

She sits down at her table
Admiring the work of the latest artist being
featured

And she feels home.

- jpl

Hair

You could tell how she was feeling
by her hair
You'd see her with bangs one day
and you'd know that that day something
happened that made her feel like she needed a
change
Not a drastic one, but just enough
If her hair was up in an unintentional messy bun
It meant she had things on her mind and couldn't
be bothered to brush it
All of a sudden you see her with a pixie cut and
knew that something big had happened
And when it was so long that it reached her
bottom
You could tell she was trying to hide something
Her hair told many things
But you'd never know what it really was

- jpl

Winter Wonderland

There was this one Christmas when my whole
family was gathered around the living room
It was so rare for all of us to be in the same room
Not getting distracted with a movie, or Where
we weren't getting berated and verbally abused
by our dad
This morning was completely serene Almost
blissful

My dad got out his guitar and he was just
playing it
We had a song book of Christmas songs so old
we had to dust the cobwebs off Because it was in
the coffee table drawer for who knows how long
I just remember that I didn't even know of its
existence until this very moment

He turned it to a page with this song called
"Winter Wonderland"
First, he was just strumming the guitar strings,
but then he began singing
It was so rare for him to sing unless we were in
the car listening to The Beatles

I was moved
I joined in, and then my sister
Even my brother was tapping his foot to the beat
The strangest reaction of all?
My mom
She was silent — something she never usually
does unless she's anxious or scared
But she just looked so peaceful and content
clapping along
Watching us with the biggest smile on her face

It was the first Christmas that was ever like that

It was also the last.

- jpl

But

You never wanted to take a picture with us
But you were always the one behind the camera
You never wanted to come to the party with us
But you always dropped us off
You never went to church with us
But you always told us we should go
You never went to any of my tennis games
But you would drop me off at the courts,
when I wanted to practice at 6 in the morning
You never told us how much you loved us
But we know you did

- jpl

Secrets

There is no appropriate time for a secret to be
told
It could be willingly or
It can be the slip of a tongue
It can be in the darkest corner of a room during a
party
Or during dinner at your favorite Thai place over
pad see yew
It could be when you're inebriated
Because a drunken mind speaks a sober heart
But one thing about secrets remain the same
That they're actually not a secret at all

- jpl

Things Fall Apart

She doesn't know why
She waits to get new things
Only replacing them
When they've completely fallen apart
She did it with her glasses
Her shoes
Her clothes
Her bags
She even did it with
Herself

- jpl

To The Man In My Room

I hope you enjoyed the show
As you watched my naked body
Slumbering on my mattress on the floor

I hope you found whatever
you were looking for
As you spilled the contents of my purse
on the floor
And I hope you use the lunch money
that my mom slipped under the door

I hope you felt relieved
after you
relieved yourself
on my purple floral duvet

and hope you know
my hysterical screams that followed after
you left

still haunt me to this day

-jpl

Those Cries

Those cries
The kind that start from seeing
a sad/happy part in a movie
But then, turns into something more
A gut wrenching cry
One you've been holding in
for who knows how long
And suddenly, you can't stop
So you let the tears fall
and begin to sob uncontrollably
Beginning to pound your chest
with a clenched fist
Because your heart hurts so damn much
So much so, the sobs turn into wails
You search around the room for a tissue
but just settle using toilet paper
You dab at your eyes, nose and cheeks
Noticing the black residue from your mascara
You look at yourself in the mirror
Sighing heavily
Then you stop just as suddenly as your started
And move on

- jpl

Codependency

I’ve been in pain so much of my life that it’s the
only way I know how to feel.

I don’t know what it feels like to feel safe and
loved unless it’s someone else that’s giving it to
me

And when they do I don’t receive it because it
feels like I don’t deserve it
I’m broken.
I’m broken in a world where I just don’t seem to
fit in.
And it really feels like people in my life would
be better off without me
Maybe I’m too far gone
I’ve worn a mask for so long that I don’t even
know who I am

- jpl

Not Alone But Lonely

How is it possible
To be surrounded by a room full of people
And yet,
Still feel completely alone

-jpl

Closure

It's finally gone
The last thing that resembled any kind of hope
of us getting back together
The last bit of attachment I had to you
The last part of me that was foolish enough to
think you'd love me again

It was in a purple draw string bag
In the third drawer of your clear storage tower
The one where you kept all the memories of us
Every gift that I had given you
Every memory shared
The items you said
"You could never throw away"
And while that may have been true
You had no trouble
Throwing me away did you?
So to you, I say thank you.

Thank you for the memories
Thank you for the greatest gift you've given me
And thank you for finally giving me
closure.

- jpl

Oxygen Mask

I don’t know how to take care of myself
But I know how to take care of other people

I need to take care of myself like how I take care of others

- jpl

This Too Shall Pass

Last night was a hard night
I felt close to losing myself again
Not physically, just this version of myself that
I've grown proud of
I was tired, worried, and anxious
I could feel past self-destructive habits and
coping mechanisms rising to the surface

I'm handling situations and occurrences a lot
better through therapy, self-analyzation, and
especially journaling
But that doesn't mean I don't still regress
sometimes
And that's okay

Because as much as it hurts right now
As much it may be hard to see past this point
I know this too shall pass
These feelings of insecurity, inadequacy, and
negativity will also pass
And even this state I'm in
These feelings I'm feeling
Is still me healing

- jpl

The In Between

The "in between" is such a hard place to be in. That place where you know you are transforming into the person you were always meant to be, but are still so desperately trying to hold on to the person you once where. Whether it be out of self doubt, fear, anxiety; you can't quite seem to step both feet out the door. I feel like my whole life I've tried to fit into this box that people have put me in. Or rather, I've put myself in out of expectations I felt like I had to meet. But that box looks different to so many people, because there are so many versions of ourselves that are created as everyone's perception of us are different.

As outspoken as I am, there are so many words I forbid to leave my lips for fear of hurting someone's feelings or shattering this reality that was so perfectly crafted, so much so, I started to believe it. There are so many things I want to do, but don't because of my unyielding fear of failure and rejection. Not just from the action itself, but also that of loved ones thinking I've "changed."

But what is life without change? Who are we without change? We as a human species are always meant to evolve, each and every season of our lives. I honestly feel like we can keep being ourselves, keeping the most integral part of our core that keeps us, "us," while still leaving room to grow each day into the person we were always meant to be.

Honestly, sometimes you just have to say "fuck it," and do what you want. The people that love you, will stay. And the people who aren't happy with you trying to be your most authentic self are better to let go.

So hey, this is me. Still the same Jocelyn, but constantly changing; constantly growing. Who are you?

- jpl

Voice

Use it
To move mountains
To break down walls
To reveal problems
To formulate solutions

Use it
With purpose
With integrity
With intention

But most importantly,
Use it with action

- jpl

On Writing

I don't know what I want to write
I just know that I do
I want to write.
It's the only thing that helps make me feel truly
better
When it feels like the world is coming down on
me
That all the feelings inside me are about to burst
The only thing that helps is grabbing a pen and
piece of paper
And writing everything down
It's how I get clarity
When nothing seems to make sense
Writing is when I feel most like myself

- jpl

Growth Spurts

Epiphanies and revelations
New found wisdom I feel the need to share this light with others
Little to no sleep,
No appetite
Bursts of motivation
And I complete the things
That have been on my to-do list for so long
I become a better person
The person I was always meant to become
Each day
Leveling up
Saying goodbye to what does not serve me anymore
Coming out of hibernation
Because I had been on autopilot for so long
After being so numb
I finally come to my senses
This is me.

- jpl

What Is Life?

Life is growing.
Life is where you never stop learning,
And always take moments and opportunities to
become a better version of yourself.
Life is playing make-pretend with my daughter
Heart-to-Heart conversations with mom
Being with my family and watching our kids
grow
It's reading a book, watching a movie
It's writing, in all shapes and forms
It's coffee and spicy ahi donburis
Or staying up late with friends, playing games
and laughing at the stupidest things
It's cracking jokes with my coworkers
It's love and the butterflies you get when you
start talking to someone
And, it's also heartbreak when you realize you
need to let someone go
It's fleeting moments with strangers on the street
And random acts of kindness
Life is so messy, but so beautiful
So beautiful.

- jpl

I am

I am peace
I am love
I am light
I am free.

- jpl

www.ingramcontent.com/pod-product-compliance
Lightning Source LLC
Chambersburg PA
CBHW051755130826
49812CB00033B/1158
* 9 7 8 9 3 5 7 4 4 2 7 6 3 *